50

DAYS OF
PROPHETIC
INSPIRATION

KECHA CHAMBERS

LOVE CLONES
publishing

Love Clones Publishing
www.lcpublishing.net

Printed in the United States of America

First Printing, 2016

ISBN: 978-0692665626

Publishers:
Love Clones Publishing
Dallas, TX 75205
www.lcpublishing.net

DEDICATION

I dedicate this book to my Heavenly Father who gifted me and predestined me for greatness.

To my Apostolic Father Apostle Robbie C. Peters thank you for empowering me and believing in me.

<u>PREFACE</u>

It is my desire that everyone who reads this book will be inspired and determined to believe in themselves and to know how special they are.

This book was written for you to let you know God has you on His mind!

Through divine inspiration of the Holy Spirit, I penned these words to uplift and point you in the direction of hope.

Allow the daily inspirations to permeate your spirit, that they may resound at the right moment to push you past what you may be feeling and press you into His presence.

Read this book knowing that whatever state you find yourself in, it is God's desire that you be encouraged and inspired to continue your journey in Him.

Be blessed

Prophetic Word For Day 1
CONFIGURE

God is saying, that He is about to do some configuration within you for a specific purpose.

"There are some components within you that need to be reconfigured so you can adapt to the plan I have for you. This design is tailor made to fit your personality, which I blew into you from the beginning.

I am reconstructing your ears to hear in a manner where you hear, and my voice is so distinct that you will only follow my commands. You will be able to hear through the chattering and the whispering. Distraction will be at a minimum because I am training your ears to hear only my voice. I have shaped your ear to hear what the Spirit is saying so you can receive the prepared things that I have for you.

I am reforming your mind to think like Christ. You cannot say you have the mind of Christ and still act like a man. As a man thinketh, so is he. You will become what you think. Renew your mind, think like Christ and become a new creation. Your mind is configured to reject a lie and accept the truth, to dispel doubt and activate faith.

I am reconfiguring your heart so that you can let go of the pain and the past. Your heart is the strongest muscle I have created in you. You can let it go! You can forgive! You can love again! You can trust people again! Your heart is configured to love unconditionally and it is supported by the King's hand. I know how to turn your heart whichever way I will. Your heart can bear the load!

I am reforming your eyes to have spiritual perception and conception. You will not be ignorant of what I am doing in your life. You will see the plans unfolding as you look in the direction of your purpose. Keep your eyes on me says the Lord for I am working a work in you to help you hope again. I am opening your eyes of understanding and enlightening you to hidden truths about your future. Behold, newness is coming, increase is coming and restoration is coming.

Prophetic Word For Day 2
MOMENTUM

God says it is time to pick up the pace. There is to be no slacking in this hour.

"I want you to enter 2015 running and putting your hand to the plough. I am creating moments for you where you have to maximize this moment. This momentum is going to carry you through the New Year."

Momentum is simply the force or speed of movement that carries an object to its final destination. If you want to break through, you need to have a certain amount of momentum.

God is sending you a power surge of faith to assure a victory. I hear the Lord saying, "I am causing that which has held back your momentum to be identified this hour so you can thrust forward and rise up again".

"The moment you get in the race a fresh wind will be given you to finish the race. The moment in which you presently reside is the key to your advancement. Do not miss the moment to move for it is the momentum to propel you forward into your new season of plenty."

"The Lord says it's time to gain momentum. Anything that has momentum is very difficult to stop. The more momentum you gain the more territory you can take."

God will be moving on us! Will we respond to Him? We must not allow the voices of fear, unbelief and doubt to stop us from advancing. The violent are taking the Kingdom of Heaven by force. We are under the impulse or driving force, of a King. We must gain momentum now!

Momentum will cause you to wax strong in spirit and be bold to speak to a mountain and see it move. The Lord of the Breakthrough is the force behind your momentum. As you gain momentum, the breakers anointing will destroy everything in its path! Let us Gain Momentum!

Prophetic Word For Day 3
ADVANCE

Know how properly to engage with God in order to advance the Kingdom. God is advancing his people into a new place we have never been before. We are positioned beneath the Heavens that have been opened by the very hand of God. We are now standing under an unrestricted Heaven.

Now is the time for advancing and accelerating. You shall experience new levels in God to advance and accelerate you in your personal life, family, businesses, church and community.

God is going to turn things around so fast that nothing or no one around you will look familiar. God is advancing his favor for birthing, establishing and building new Kingdom projects, relationships and businesses.

Do not procrastinate for this is an open door

and a time for advancement! Keep your eyes on God and the Word for in this we will experience a shift that will propel and catapult us in the flow of unexpected blessings.

Prophetic Word For Day 4
POSSESSION

I the Lord say, It Is Time To Possess the Promises I have for you! This is your time and this is your season of blessings to flow in your life. You have waited a long time to take hold of my promises, but the wait is over."

We are in a season of possessing the promise. We are in a time of crossing over from one season into another, from the wilderness into the Promised Land.

As we are in transition, things around us become unsettling. The spiritual landscape is changing as we move into unfamiliar territory. The spirit of fear will try to dominate us and try to keep us from possessing the promise.

Overcome the fear that lies within you with the power you possess. Fear cannot stop you, but it can delay you from possessing the promise. "There is a set time to get your inheritance," says the Lord. "Pace yourself and walk through the open door and into your promise."

"There are divine patterns I have established in my Word that are for the purposes of identifying the road to possessing the promises. Follow the patterns of the prophetic words, the progressive revelations and the empowering biblical truths I have spoken in your ears through my sent ones. It will lead you right to the promise to possess it."

"Don't deviate from my plans; I will not fail you. You will possess every promise I have promised you. I am not limited by your time, but I have brought you into my season. A day is as a thousand years and a thousand years as a day. "This is the appointed time and it shall suddenly appear."

Prophetic Word For Day 5
PRAISE

Praise the Lord oh ye people! Praise Him at the gate! Praise Him in the courts! Praise Him in the sanctuary! Praise Him from the rising of the sun to going down of the same! Praise Him!

Praise Him above your circumstances. Praise Him in the midst of a storm. Exalt Him. In spite of everything you have been through you should Praise Him. In spite of your test, you must praise Him. In spite of your mess, your praise should be unrestricted.

God has been there through it all. He never left you nor forsook you. He deserves your praise. He wants your praise. Your praise should be designed to fit the King of Kings. He is the amazing God, so your praise should not just be what you do but why, when and how you praise for He is worthy of our praise.

Praise your way right out of that place of

despair. Praise your way right into the presence of the Lord. Praise paves a way to the Holy One who inhabits your words of thanksgiving. Thankfulness makes room for Him to visit you. Your holy visitation is contingent upon your praise to the one who responds to your call.

Prophetic Word For Day 6
PROCEED

I hear the Lord say, "My word has preceded me. I sent my word forth to establish some things in your life in order that you may be filled with every kind of provision so you can increase more and more."

"My word preceded the verdict of that miracle for which you've been asking me. Wait for it, it shall come to pass, and it will not tarry says the Lord. Stop worrying about what could have been and realize what you have now. It's better than what's been."

"My word paved the way for your blessings and it has an expected end. Your latter will be greater. You will reap where you have not sown. You will prosper in the place I have sent you. You will not lose a thing. I have prospered your hands to be blessed and to be a blessing."

"My word has gone before your prayers, and

I'm sending my host to bring you the answer. Don't cease from talking with me for my ears are attuned to your prayers. Ask and it shall be given. Ask according to my will and it is done. Ask with an upright heart and I will not withhold my pleasures from you."

"My word has preceded you and has set a hedge of protection around you to keep you from the evil that is to come. My word is more powerful than any other power and you will not be hurt. Stay in my shadow for it shall preserve your going out and coming in. Don't move anymore until my word has preceded your movement."

"It is my word that causes you to live, move and have your being. My word sets you, establishes you, guides you, prospers you, washes and cleanses you, proceeds and follows you, protects and shields you and gives you life! Never doubt my word; it never fails nor will it return to me without fulfilling my purpose. My word is who I Am, and I Am is the Word!"

Prophetic Word For Day 7
REFINE

"I hear your cries as you call out to me," says the Lord in the fiery (furnace?). Although the trials seem to multiply, I am with you through them all. Just as the refining of gold takes away impurities, the things in your life that are unacceptable shall be removed."

"The process of refining is to separate the pure from the impure. I am removing the dross from your life through the refining process. You shall be purified and worthy of double honor after this. Trust me to strengthen you as you are refined in these trying times."

God says, "I Am applying the heat; I Am blowing my fire upon you to consume the impurities. I am reestablishing my covenant with you. Don't focus on your past for it will only cause you to delay from moving into your future. You shall come through these difficult seasons on fire for me," says the Lord.

"Allow the refining process to bring all the pollutants to surface that keep you imprisoned. Trust me," says the Lord. "You will be released from the uncleanness which tries to hide within my vessels. After this, you can begin living a life of abundance."

Prophetic Word For Day 8
CONTINUE

I hear the Lord say, "Continue through adversity, continue through the pain, continue through the tears, continue when you don't understand, continue when you're in lack, continue when in abundance." I hear God say, "Just continue! "If you continue in my word," says God", I will sustain you in this season." Your ability to keep going proves to God that you are ready for the release of his hand. Don't stop moving in the things of God for it is your progression to your destiny.

When you continue you are making advanced steps to your purpose place in God. "Continuous movements," I hear the Lord say. Don't stop and take a breather; just inhale and exhale while you are moving. As you continue you will have uninterrupted accessibility to God's favor.

If you don't continue, you will cause a break

in the cycle of progression. You cause your momentum to weaken. Your persistence is compromised and you will become exhausted with trying to pick up where you stopped. Press onward, continue, advance and do business in the Kingdom.

Prophetic Word For Day 9
HOPE

Hope is the feeling that what you wanted can be obtained or that the situation will turn out for the best.

Hope shines brightest when the hour is darkest. Hope motivates when discouragement comes. Hope energizes when the body is tired. Hope gives you a new song to sing in the midst of sorrow. Hope believes when evidence can't be seen. Hope in Christ.

Hope listens for answers when no one is talking. Hope gives you strength to jump over obstacles. Hope endures hardship when you're doing it alone. Hope smiles confidently when you can't. Hope reaches for answers when no one is asking. Hope in Christ.

Hope presses toward victory when you stop looking back. Hope dares you to believe when things seems impossible. Hope is faith in seed form and faith is hope in final form. Hope in Christ.

I want you to know that whatever situation you find yourself in at this moment, there is hope. You may not be able to see or feel the hope, but it is there for you. You need to agree with God about your situation. Hope is real. So hope in Christ.

Prophetic Word For Day 10
EMBRACE

"Embrace the Holy Spirit," so says the Lord, "because I want to tell and show you many things to come."

"For my Spirit is a Comforter, Counselor, Helper, Intercessor, Advocate, Ally and a Strengthener. The Holy Spirit, whom I sent in my name, in my place to represent me and act on my behalf, will teach you all things."

"Embrace the Holy Spirit for He is the one who anoints you to do Kingdom work. You cannot operate in the Kingdom without the Spirit. He gives you power to heal, deliver and set free."

"The Holy Spirit comes to reveal those prepared things I have for you. Embrace my Spirit He is your guide to the supernatural. The Holy Spirit comes to finish the work of Christ in you. Embrace the Spirit."

Quench not the Holy Spirit!

- He will reveal the deep things of God.

- He will open the floodgates upon you.

- He will breathe fresh wind to revive you.

- He will anoint you with oil for service.

- He will fill you with holy wine.

- He will refine you with fire.

- He will give you power and authority.

I pray the Lord will send the Holy Spirit to come to you NOW. God says, "I never ignore a request, ask and it shall be given."

Prophetic Word For Day 11
FIGHT

God told me to tell you to fight. Fight for that in which you believe, for all things are possible to them that believe.

God says, "I know your struggles with your body, your mind, your marriage, your family, your children, your finances, your faith, your mistakes, your life choices, but if you fight the good fight of faith you will finish strong," says the Lord.

God says, "I have created in you a mechanism to fight so even if you want to give up you can't. Take the magnifying glass off the problem and put your eyes of faith on me because I'm the author and the finisher of your faith."

God says, "Fight until a decision is reached. Never back down to a fight. Be determined to win. Fight with intensity. Fight with force. Fight to prevail. I will finish what you started." God says, "If you're winning or have the lead in the fight I will finish it with a victory."

Prophetic Word For Day 12
BEYOND

The Lord is saying, "You have to go beyond your weakness to know your strength. You are stronger than you think. Even at your weakest moments, you are stronger because you survive it."

The Lord is saying, "In order to be made whole you have to go beyond the pain."

"As you allow My word to sustain you, you will soon be strengthened beyond your natural abilities. You will no longer be limited in your ways of thinking. You will no longer look to the wisdom of man, but you will trust the truth of My word."

Going beyond the limits you put on God will allow you to experience more divine things. Take the limits off! God is an infinite God, and there is no ending to His being. You can explore the supernatural when you go beyond the natural.

Breaking free of self-imposed limits will empower you to enjoy an amazing God beyond your imaginations. Limitations keep you complacent, comfortable and living beneath your privilege. Break-free and go beyond your biggest dream or vision and explore an unlimited passage of blessings.

God is waiting on you to go beyond your limitations. It's time to enjoy a fresh and exciting new encounter with God without limits.

Prophetic Word For Day 13
DEMONSTRATE

God says, "It's time to demonstrate that which you profess and confess. Demonstration is in order," so says the Spirit of God.

"This is the day of demonstration of my Glory. You are my people who will walk in authority, power and demonstration of My kingdom. I am releasing My Spirit upon you to demonstrate my will on earth as it is in heaven."

"You have been chosen as conduits to demonstrate miracles, signs and wonders. I want to see you speak to the mountains and mountains are moved. I am looking for you to demonstrate my strength, to run this race with patience, stand strong when the winds and waves arise, validate your faith to walk on water and not allow fear to overtake you.

Children of light release my light into areas of darkness to open the lost blinded eyes, and to turn them from darkness to light, and from the power of Satan unto God, that they may receive forgiveness of sins, and inheritance among them which are sanctified by faith that is in me," so says the Spirit of the Lord.

Demonstration is in order!

Prophetic Word For Day 14
IGNORANT

God says tell my people, "Although this is your set time for favor, and even though I am opening doors no man can shut, although I'm making room for your increase, and while I'm multiplying seeds sown, be not ignorant of Satan's devices. Be not ignorant of the sin that lieth at the door. Be not ignorant of the fiery darts thrown at you. Be not ignorant of the weapons formed. Be not ignorant of flattering tongues. Be not ignorant of the small foxes or the little leaven. For the devil's devices will make you abort or give in to his tactics."

God says, "Don't ignore your dreams. Don't ignore the truth. Don't ignore the signs. Don't ignore the quickening of the Holy Ghost. Don't ignore my voice. For I Am able to do just what I said I could do. I will prepare a table of blessing before your enemy, and the enemy will know that

I Am your God!"

Prophetic Word For Day15
FEARLESS

I hear the Lord saying, "I have not given you the spirit of fear but of love, power and a sound mind. In this next move of mine, I need my people to be fearless and bold as lions.

I am looking for those who are tenacious in spiritual warfare and who are skillful in the word. I seek those who are fearless of the enemy's tactics and will not rest until the enemy is destroyed. I search out those who will go into the enemy's camp and set the captives free.

The fearless will never retreat in adverse times. They will stand and not fear the days ahead. The lion-hearted have vision to see what is on the horizon and will not be moved by an approaching storm.

The courageous will discern false teachings and false prophets because they will recognize My voice. They will walk in a life of victory because they are Spirit led and not led by their own desires.

The valiant know how to enter into the Holy of Holies and maneuver in the realm of the spirit to attain what they need.

There is now an open door to enter into my presence in a new way.

"I have provided for you to receive my anointing without measure. There is a greater glory and a new authority available to you that you have not known before. Make yourself available," says the Lord.

Prophetic Word For Day 16
CONFESS

Confessing the Word of God over your life is like standing under a waterfall where the showers of blessings flow. You will be deluged with the promises of God abundantly. So speak God's word daily over your life, over the life of your children, over your church and over your city to experience the outpour of God's unmerited favor.

Confession of faith says to God that I trust you for the impossible. Confession of praise says to God that I thank you for the invisible. Confession of worship says to God that you are more than life to me. Daily confession of the Word of God brings loaded benefits.

Confession is good for the soul, body and spirit. When you confess the word, you are bringing God into your life, into your situation, into your hopes and into your dreams. For without God we can do nothing.

Confession of God's name connects you to the power of his name. Confessing God's word over your life enlightens you to the truth of what God says you can have. Confession of God's truth will bring you into your now. Confessing God's word is what will have the authority in our lives. Continue to confess his word and his word will illuminate brightly through you.

Prophetic Word For Day 17
SAFETY

I hear the Lord saying, "Get into the ark of safety and stay there. As my children, you must choose to stay in my safety zone. My Word will keep you in the safety zone; it will establish the boundaries to keep you from danger seen and unseen.

My Word is like the highway, which has lines that provide margins for your safety. STAY WITH IN THE LINES! Do not cross over the line. Do not merge over to lanes that have been closed off to you. Stay within the lines of purpose I have for you.

My secret place is a safety zone. My shadow is a safety zone. My Word is a safety zone. My pavilion is a safety zone. My presence is a safety zone. The blood is a safety zone. My wings are a safety zone. My hand is a safety zone and my tabernacle is a safety zone."

As the Lord speak expressively to me, He says tell my people to get in my ark of safety and stay in it.

For what's to come, being out of line may cost you everything. My safety zones will protect you from the penalty of man's sinful behavior and the rudiments of this world's system. Do not be outside of the safety zone where I can't protect you.

The Lord says tell my watchmen, "Be wise and sound the alarm. My prophets and seers have discernment and precision. My intercessors, be strategic and skillful. My people, be humble and prayerful. Though a host may encamp about you, I have you covered in the safety zone.

Prophetic Word For Day 18
PERSONAL

I hear the Lord saying, "This next blessing, your next promotion, and your next miracle is going to be personal - just for you."

God says, "You've been waiting a long time to be blessed, but this next blessing is going to be personal and tailor made to fit you!"

God said, "I am personally directing this blessing your way. You are not going to miss it. It's not going to be delayed or denied because I Am the Director and I will send your blessing directly to you."

God says, "Your next miracle is intended for you. No, it is not a mistake, it is not an error; you deserve this miracle. You have trusted that I can do it, you have faith in me to perform and it's my intention to manifest it.

As it relates to you individually, I AM favoring you because you are my own. I AM commanding my angels to visit you to bestow honor, blessings and glory to you."

I hear God say, "I'm giving special care and attention to how I'm going to bless you. I will not send man to bless you for I am dealing with your blessing by myself. Therefore, there will be neither mistakes nor misunderstanding of the way it shall be done.

Prophetic Word For Day 19
ASK

The Lord says, "You have not, because you asked not, and you asked amiss. You've asked according to your wants and not your need.

God says, "I've commanded you to seek the Kingdom first and all my righteousness and all your wants I will add to you."

God says, "Your asking has been in vain, because you asked for the wrong things. You did not ask in faith of a divine promise; nor with thankfulness for past mercies; nor with submission to the will of God; nor with a right motive to do well to others, nor to give to the poor for the lending to God, nor in the interest of Christ."

God says, "Now begin to ask according to my will and you shall receive. Ask according to your faith and it shall be done unto you. Ask according to my will and I will hear you. Ask according to the power within and I will exceed your expectations. Ask anything in my Son's name and I will perform it."

Prophetic Word For Day 20
REQUIREMENT

As I seek him for the word of the day, I heard the Lord ask me; what does the LORD our God require to advance and occupy? Here is the answer:

1. Fear the LORD your God;
2. To walk in all His ways and to love Him;
3. To serve the LORD your God with all your heart and with all your soul, and to keep the commandments of the LORD and His statutes which He commands you;
4. Seek the kingdom of God and all his righteousness.
5. Pray without ceasing.
6. Walk in agreement.
7. Meditate on the word day and night;
8. To love, forgive and be obedient;
9. To have faith;

10. Be sober and vigilant;

It is our requirement to be faithful to God. Keeping his commandments is not an option in the kingdom; it's a requirement. There are requirements needed to change your whole life and that's being willing and obedient.

God is requiring us to live holy, conquer fear, submit to one another, walk by faith, be made whole, study his word in order to advance the kingdom and occupy until he comes.

Prophetic Word For Day 21
MOVEMENT

We are in the greatest time for another powerful move of God. God is sending His Spirit and His Word again upon the face of the earth as he did in the beginning.

"In the beginning I sent my Spirit to fill the earth with everything it needed to shape it, to fulfill it and give it light."

We are in the last day revival where God's Spirit and Word are moving upon the earth causing it to bring forth the fruit. It will be the greatest revival this world has ever seen! The gifts of the Spirit will be perfected. The ministry gifts will be flowing and moving in this earth.

The Holy Ghost will move in the churches during this last day revival and we will see the wonders of the Lord. The Holy Ghost is moving upon the set gifts in the house where their works will be tried. Moreover, the Sons of God, those that are led by the Spirit of God will be endowed with the Holy Ghost without measure.

"This movement is for mature sons and daughters in whom I can show myself strong. They will operate in the swift strategic movement as the Spirit breath blows upon the earth. There shall be a great shaking of the earth as of an earthquake breaking up the fallow of the ground."

The Spirit of God is moving, and you better get in the wind to be in the flow of God. For the Four Winds of God are coming and it will destroy everything in its path that's not like God.

Prophetic Word For Day 22
NEW

New is something that is fresh, a new object,
new in quality and new in condition.[1]

God says that in order for him to do
something new in your life you have to get rid of
the old. I hear the Lord saying, "How long will
you think like that? How long are you going to
hold on to that? How long will it be like that? Let
go of that old thinking, old habit, and old ways
because I want to do something new in and
through you."

I hear the Lord say, "It won't always be like
that; your latter will be greater."

Trust him in letting go of the old, and he will be
faithful bringing in the new.

"There are many blessing I want to bestow
upon you," says the Lord, "but your lack of faith is
holding it up. Fear is not of me," says the Lord.

"Fear will keep you in the old and faith will bring you into the new."

Prophetic Word For Day 23
ALIGNMENT

The Apostles have given us many prophetic words such as "the year of the open door," and in the beginning of the New Year, Apostle Sharon said this was a season of fresh oil and we are a distribution center.

Now God is prophetically aligning all the prophecies that have been spoken over our lives to come together so he can perform it.

Before the year is out the Holy Spirit will align God's people with His purpose. This positioning will be brought by way of revelation of God's plan for individuals. These revelations will come through dreams, visions, prophetic words, signs and wonders.

We must be on alert so that the opportunities for alignment are not missed. You will be adjusted and brought into spiritual positioning, to go through the door that is being opened to you.

Spiritual doors will open in this season that will bring you into a new spiritual landscape. It will become a place of elevation, a higher place than you have ever been before. God is changing the scenery.

Prophetic Word For Day 24
PREPARE

Prepare means to put things or oneself in readiness, so get ready: Start arranging or rearranging your life to get ready for God's release of provision for the vision in your life. Whatever is out of order or in disarray in your life will not make room for you to receive God's provision.

You've got to begin preparing and making ready for the expected and unexpected blessing of the Lord.

Prepare beforehand for the coming of the Lord, for when he visits you will be ready to receive and conceive.

Blessing is approaching, promotions are approaching, breakthroughs are approaching and uncommon favor is approaching. Will you be ready?

This is going to be an eventful 2016 for you, but you have to be prepared for increase, the outpour, the blessing, and the abundance.

Preparation is necessary and essential, and it shows God you are ready and conditioned for the greater that is coming.

GET READY! GET READY! GET READY!

Prophetic Word For Day 25
BURY

Bury means to put in the ground and cover with earth.[1]

No longer are you to hide that thing which hinders you, stops you or silences you. You are to bury that thing by putting it in the ground and covering it with the earth never to rise again.

Do not carry something you know is dead into the next year. Anything that is dead needs to be buried. Dead things are weighty and become burdensome or troublesome.

Free yourself from the deadly burdens that are killing you spiritually. You may have a burden but it's not your burden. Don't let it become a weight; the only weight you are to carry is the weight of God's glory.

Prophetic Word For Day 26
PERIOD

Period means the point of completion of a round of time or of the time during which something lasts or happens.[1]

God says to be not weary in well doing for we shall reap if we faint not. There are some things that are coming to an end in your life for it has reached its point of completion. It's Reaping time!

The bible says the end of a thing is better than the beginning. Despise not the end of a thing for its more profitable for you. Time is up for the enemy causing havoc in your life.

God says it is time for your harvest to last. It's time for your increase to last. It's time for your healing to last. It's time for your deliverance to last. It's time for miracles to happen. It's time for signs and wonders to start happening.

Decree this with me:

- It will last period.
- It will happen period.
- I will not lack period.
- I will live abundantly period.
- I deserve it period.
- God will not slack period.
- God will period.
- God promised period.
- God favored me period.
- God loves me period.

Prophetic Word For Day 27
UP

Up means to or at a higher point or degree, as of rank, size, value, pitch, loudness, brightness, maturity, or speed.[1]

We have been down so long that we can't go anywhere else but up. We're getting up from this pain, disappointment, failure, depression, lack, hurt, betrayal, lies, and abuse. It can't hold us down any longer.

I heard God say, that we're going up from here!

We're going up in rank, we're going up in size, we're going up in value, we're going up in pitch, and we're going up in loudness, brightness, maturity and speed!

God always requires man to come up, go up, and stand up and to look up to receive his provisions, his revelation and see the manifestation of signs and wonders.

So let us be built up, let us wake up, let's stay prayed up and let us mount up and watch God rise up and pay up.

Prophetic Word For Day 28
CHANGE

Change is a transformation or modification; alteration.[1]

Many are experiencing the transformation process where God is changing your form, shape and even your appearance. When you come out of this process you won't look the same, feel the same nor act the same. The very essence of all that you are is being transformed.

Some are experiencing the process of modifications where your DNA is changing. God is infusing more of his DNA into you, which is changing your physical character, growth and development. There shall be glory and elevation after this process.

Others are experiencing the process of alterations where God is adjusting you, adjusting your size, expanding you, and stretching you to fit the mandate, assignment or the plan. You are going through phases. God is taking you from faith to faith, from strength to strength and glory to glory.

God is doing something new in us to change us for the better to receive what's coming. Don't fight change; if you do, in the transformation process you'll become disfigured; your distinction and anointing will be unrecognizable. In the modification process, you will lose your identity and become double-minded and in the alteration process, you will be in a maze always repeating the same cycle of life and never reaching new heights or r dimensions in God.

Therefore, if we are to advance and occupy, change is necessary for progression. Although you may lose some good things while you're changing, you also gain some better things in the change.

Prophetic Word For Day 29
REST

Rest means to lay or place for rest, ease, or support[1]

God is saying, "Whatever you rest or place on me, you are laying the weight on me, and I have the capacity to support it."

God said, "It was me supporting you that kept you from giving up. It was I supporting you that kept you from losing your mind. It was me supporting you that preserved you, so you don't look like what you've been through."

God said, "Lay it to rest, all your burdens, problems, issues, circumstances on me because I can carry the weight of it. In this season, I am bearing the weight of your burdens so your journey will be easier."

"As you lay aside the weight, you will then feel the release of it from your heart and mind and your shoulders."

In this season of rest build up your strength, build up your endurance and build up your faith, because in your next trial or test you will have the ability to bear the weight."

Prophetic Word For Day 30
FINISH

Finish means to bring (something) to an end or to completion; complete[1]

God said do not let any unfinished business go into the New Year. God says, "In this New Year, I am accelerating you, for you are behind on the prepared things I have for you. Some of which was your fault but some of it was the enemy fault."

God said if you finish what you started, He would cause what you complete to prosper and multiply for a great harvest for you. God says, "How you end this year is how you are going to begin in the New Year, and I am going to begin in this year the way you finished in the old year."

Now this is Prophet Kecha speaking and not the Lord. If you began a project this year, finish it. If you were working on being healthier, finish it.

If you started praying more finish it. If you started working on getting out of debt, finish it. If it is your desire to spend more time with family, finish it. If you started to be more spiritual, finish it etc.

What I am saying is complete what you started so your new beginning will pick up where it left off. You'll be more productive when you finish not what you started. Focus on the journey and not the destination and you will probably culminate the task.

Prophetic Word For Day 31
HEAL

Heal means to make healthy, whole, or sound; restore to health.[1]

God says to tell my church that I am healing them. I am healing them from all emotional, physical, relational psychological, financial and mental wounds.

God said, "You have been in the fight too long and have suffered injuries that only I can heal." God says, "I am taking you out of the battle and I'm binding up your wounds."

God commanded me to send the word to your emotional health, physical health, relational health, psychological health, financial health and mental health. You have lost a lot of sleep, money, strength and time, but "I will restore," says the Lord.

"I have put you back in the process of healing

so the pain of the loss will become numb. You will heal correctly. Stop worrying about it; it's my turn now to take away the hurt or misfortune."

"I'm calling you to this place of healing, for where I'm taking this church no pain of any kind can go there. Your health is being restored!"

Prophetic Word For Day 32
ALERT

Alert means to be fully aware and attentive; wide-awake; keen: having an alert mind.[1]

God is saying, "In this season you will be more aware of the things I am doing in your life. No longer will you miss the blessings of the Lord. No longer will you miss the promises I have for you."

"I am giving you an alert mind if you can keep your eyes stayed on me. Do not look to the left or to the right, for the things I have prepared for you are straight ahead."

"Your alertness will make you aware of impeding danger. The enemy will not catch you off guard anymore if you stay watchful."

"Be alert concerning your surroundings, for I the Lord will show up anywhere. Some of you were not alert when I came unto you when you called, therefore I was there waiting on you to let me in."

"Now I AM has grabbed your attention. Move quickly when I come, for I will not tarry to give you my good pleasures. You will be alert when I am moving, you will know when to pray, you will know when to fight and you will know when to be still and see me avenge my people."

Be alert, be watchful, be vigilant, be on guard, be observant and watch your surroundings God is going to show up anywhere.

Prophetic Word For Day 33
SETTLE

Settle means resolve or reach an agreement about (an argument or problem).[1]

God says you are about to reach an agreement about those things you have up before him.

God says He is sorting out some things to work for your good. God says when an agreement has been reached you will be clear on which settlement to take.

I hear God say, "Don't SETTLE for LESS than you deserve, for I have set right the dispute, and I have rectified the problem.

You deserve to be happy. You deserve to free. You deserve to be rich. You deserve to have peace. God says, "I'm even causing some legal matters in the spirit realm to be settled." God says, "The enemy has prolonged your healing, prosperity, provision, deliverance and your peace with disputes in Heaven," but the Lord says, "I'm SETTLING IT right now."

God says it has been determined that you are about to get everything you deserve for Grace and Favor has fixed it!

In addition, guess what? If God said it, that settles it!

Prophetic Word For Day 34
RESISTANCE

Resistance is the ability NOT to be affected by something, especially adversely.[1]

I decree that this trial will not affect you and make you give in to adversity. Your resistance of the devil will make him flee. Therefore, I command you to resist the enemy's fiery darts and stand brave against these adverse attempts.

You have been given power to resist the devil through the power of prayer, through the eyes of faith, fighting with the whole armor of God and with humility. Your resistance to the devil and his tactics is through your submission to God. Yield to God not the adversary!

It is the enemy's job to cause hell in your life, but when you are going through, keep going, don't stop! Your resistance to the fire puts the fire out.

Prophetic Word For Day 35
CHANCE

Chance means a risk; a possibility or probability of anything happening.[1]

Life is all about taking risks for the possibility of something great happening in your life. Don't stop taking chances in life, for if you do, you stop the opportunity of God making that thing happen for you. Risks in life may cause you to win or lose but you will never know if you never take the chance. Some of you all are at the brink of winning, but are afraid to take the risk.

Take another chance to live again, laugh again, trust again, hope again, pray again, believe again, forgive again, breathe again and begin again, because in the end we only regret the chances we didn't take.

Prophetic Word For Day 36:
COMPLETE

Complete means having all parts and elements; lacking nothing; entire; whole.[1]

You will be complete in every area of your life according to the predestination and the timing of God. The part that you thought was missing was held by God to complete you at the very moment you were about to give up.

God says, "You fell apart and lost some parts, but I am calling for the wind of the Spirit to bring those parts back together. You will be made whole again, nothing broken, nothing missing." God says, "All things are working for your good. You are now at a place of Rehoboth, for I have made room for you."

God's says, "This room shall be a great supplier for all your needs, so lack has no place in your room. Great reward is set up in this room to furnish what you have desired. Because you have stood the test, kept the faith, obeyed my word and have been a witness, I have expanded the dimensions of your room."

"I Am sending my angelic host to go to and fro all over the earth to complete the work I began, to bless and prosper you. This shall be a season of reaping to fulfill your petition that you have requested of me. I have taken your little and multiplied it for you to be blessed and be a blessing."

"At the completion of your test you will possess and occupy your inheritance for you and children," says the Lord. I am bringing wholeness to your broken places. The voids in your life will be filled with the refreshing waters of the Spirit. The realization of your faith will walk you into the manifestation of what you believe."

God says to tell you, "No longer will you go outside of you to get what you need but you will access the water within you." God says, "I Am breaking your water bag, and you shall now bring forth. You are at the completion of the set time to birth out that with which I have impregnated you. I hear God say, "You're on schedule. There will be no more delays."

Prophetic Word For Day 37
MAINTAIN

With every blessing or gift you receive from God, there is the responsibility to maintain it. Do not lose your zeal or fervor while God is blessing. The same fervency you had before the blessing, you should maintain that same zeal.

God said, "You maintain your hair, nails, wardrobe and anything else that is outside of you, but have you maintained the inner man. It is important to maintain spiritual growth so you will mature and be built up to operate in the Kingdom as sons of God. There are no maintenance-free-gifts or blessings."

Your deliverance, healing, salvation, divine relationships, spiritual gifts, grace gifts, spirituality, mental stability and your soul, all need to be maintained in order to prosper, be fruitful, to multiply, to subdue and to have dominion and authority.

The Lord said, "Consider a car; in order for the car to function properly you have to do some maintenance: such as change the oil, rotate tires, calibrate, fix broken lights and keep it clean.

So shall you consider your temple? Have you checked your oil since your last test and trial? Are you low or does it need to be changed? Maybe you are operating off of dirty oil and it's causing you to run differently, slowly, and hesitantly or burning a lot of gas. Maybe you are too tired to progress.

Are your headlights burned out so that you can't even see the plans God has for you so you stay where you are? Some of you need to re-calibrate; your gauges are off balance and you are going too fast and getting ahead of God or you need to go faster to catch up with God.

God wants us to maintain our spirituality so we will not quickly give in to the wiles of the devil. Neither does He desire us to malfunction when we are low on oil and the lights burn out.

Let's do a maintenance check.

- Check your oil - are you being led by the Spirit?
- Check your faith - are you hearing the Word and doing it?
- Check your lights - are you hiding it so that men can't see and God can't be glorified?
- Check you love walk - are you constantly being offended?
- Check your prayer life - have you ceased from praying, and has your incense gone out?

I hear the Lord say that low maintenance equals low performance.

Prophetic Word For Day 38
UNDERSTAND

Understanding is the ability to perceive and discern the time and seasons in your life in order to apply wisdom to make the right moves.[1]

Understanding your times and seasons will help prevent you from making many futuristic mistakes. It will keep you from being impulsive and making unwise decisions in your life. Discern your season, and you will know if it is the right time for you to go through the open door or to shut the door.

When it's your time to prosper God will make everything fall into place. All of the right doors will open for you and all the right people will be there to help you succeed. In this period you must perceive where you are going, who God is going to use to get you there and what you must do when you get there.

When you don't understand the times and seasons of your life, you will likely run into various walls, road blocks, obstacles, resistance, closed doors, insurmountable pressure, and a lot of unfavorable conditions. God's seasons are favorable.

There are red flags and protective barriers that are set in place by God to protect you from stepping outside his timing. Sometimes it's not the season for marriage, ministry, children or business. God is not a killjoy; you will definitely come into prophetic fulfillment.

You must comprehend there is a set time and a set season for everything that the Lord has in store for you in life.   So that your progress in God will not be hindered, you must have the spirit of Issachar to understand the times and seasons.

Prophetic Word For Day 39
ENTER

I hear the Lord say, "You may enter in, for I have given you access to the Kingdom. This realm has unlimited resources and endless portals to an open heaven. Enter my sanctuary: It is beautiful and loaded with benefits for my children. That which you seek is laid up in heavenly places."

"The entrance to the unfathomed is at your reach. Press forward and go beyond the place of comfort and experience me like never before. Behold a door of hope has been opened for you. Enter at your own risk. You are entering a season of breakthrough, full recovery and unobstructed doors."

Those who have not grown weary and have contended for the faith will make a full recovery. You will enter a new life and walk out of a life of limitations and restriction through the vast door

God has set before you into a place of Kingdom power and provision.

This access of the open door is so that no man can prevent you from entering; neither will any situation be able to hinder you from walking through. Approach this door with great expectation, hesitant not to enter in due to frustration and distrust in your hearts.

Many of you have said inwardly that you have heard this before but you have not experienced it personally, but I say to you, as you remain steadfast you will behold what your eyes have not seen and what the Lord has prepared for you in this hour.

Prophetic Word For Day 40
THANKFUL

God says, "If you want to be in my will, give thanks. Thankfulness commands heaven to establish my will on earth." God says, "I want you to be thankful in everything and for everything."

God says, "I want you to be thankful every day in this season for I have given you many things. I have poured out great favor upon you. I have given my abiding presence among you."

God says, "Be thankful. I've shown up in the house when you asked me to, and I did many signs and wonders in your worship experience. I have lifted the spirit of heaviness from you and caused the spirit of grace to rule and abound."

God says, "Be thankful. I have said that I would establish your going out and your coming in. I said, there is no sick or feeble among you. I said your house is filled with every kind of provision and you shall increase. I said you are a distribution center, and I will hasten my word to perform it."

God says, "I shall do even greater than before. I am asking you to be an example of gratefulness and thankfulness in all things. I have given you my word, and I will accomplish it and prosper it, and it will not return void."

Prophetic Word For Day 41
SUDDEN

Sudden means happening, coming, made or done quickly, without warning or unexpectedly.[1]

As you wait upon the Lord in this time of your life with prayer and thanksgiving, God is going to come quickly on your behalf and bless you with something you were not expecting.

Your blessings are coming. Be not weary in well doing and keep pressing toward the things of the kingdom for God is into adding and multiplying to your life without warning.

Divine things are happening all around. God is creating an atmosphere that is fit for his sons and daughters and will glorify him. The unforeseen will be made known in days to come, so be expecting an opportunity, surprise or occurrence to take place.

Prophetic Word For Day 42
RELEASE

Release - to free from confinement,
bondage, obligation, pain etc., let go.[1]

God is releasing you from the bondage that has fastened you to a lie that says you can't be free from that sickness, debt, pain or the past. This bondage has held on to you long enough. I command those chains to broken off you NOW.

God has set in place liberty for his people where no restraints can hinder them in their process of letting go. Your past cannot control your present or your future, for the God of the breakthrough has loosed you from the past.

You are free to move around in the Kingdom of Heaven and explore the goodness of the Lord. God is releasing portals in heaven for those who are not confined to material blessings. "Those that are seekers of the Kingdom and righteousness I

Am releasing upon you not just what you need but also what you want."

This is the year of the release, so be ready to experience freedom from that thing that held you captive in your mind, in the same cycle of lack, which kept you from experiencing the new season. Say this out loud: "I Am breaking free and entering into the newness of life without restraints."

Prophetic Word For Day 43
MORE

More - something of greater importance[1]

God told me to tell you, you are more than that one mistake. You are more than that failed relationship. You are more than those wrong choices. You are more than that bad habit. "You are more to me," says God, "because you are of great importance to me."

"Your past mistakes, failures, wrong choices or bad habits don't outweigh who you are to me. You are my chosen generation, my royal priesthood, and my peculiar people. When I created you, I saw that you were good. You are more than my creation; you are my reflection and the image of my deity."

"You are so important to me that I blew my DNA in you so you can think like me, love like me, create like me, have dominion like me and most of all to be holy like me. You are my heirs and joint heirs with Jesus Christ thy Redeemer, and the Greater One is living on the inside of you."

"No more low thinking, average living or having enough to get by, for I Am giving you more power to get wealth. I am giving you more wisdom to maintain your prosperity. I am giving you more of my honor to impact nations. I am giving you more of my Spirit to live a productive and fruitful life."

Prophetic Word For Day 44
LIVE

Live - to have life, to experience or enjoy to the full.[1]

The Lord said to ask my people a question. "What are you waiting on to live? I have given you everything that pertains to life and godliness. Go ahead and live! Live life to the fullest." Living is not simply existing, but continuing in life in a specified manner according to God's design.

God designed heaven and earth for us to live in abundance, peace and joy. Go ahead and live! Don't allow age, lack of resources or approval of man to stop you from living. Life is on the inside of you and is ready to burst forth as you release the living water that flows from your belly. Go ahead and live!

I come to inspire you to live life by God's design and not only live life but also speak life, for the Word of God is alive. I speak health and wealth over your life. I speak prosperity and peace over your life. I speak healing and deliverance over your life. I speak wholeness and completeness over your life. Now live!

Prophetic Word For Day 45
IMMEDIATELY

Immediately- without lapse of time, without delay, instantly, at once.[1]

There is going to be an immediate turn around for you because you stood the test of time. Instantaneous blessings of the Lord are going to overtake you. As soon as the test came, you immediately begin to give thanks in it, for you knew the good, acceptable and perfect will of God for your life.

God said, make your request known unto him and he will respond without delay. Your blessing is on the way as soon as you petition the Lord, for you have made God your refuge. I decree no more delay or lapse of time of your promises, for they are presently being released into your storehouses.

You're going to get up immediately from this lack, famine, drought and waiting. Effortlessly you're going to be readily exposed to El-Shaddai, the God of more than enough. God is hastening his word to perform this promise in your life. No more long waiting for what belongs to you, God is expeditiously moving on your behalf.

The Prophetic Word For Day 46
PROOF

Proof - able to withstand, successful in not being overcome.[1]

Your demonstration of standing in the evil day and doing all to withstand, has proven that you are an overcomer. The devices of the adversary were impenetrable, therefore unable to move you out of position. Your position of faith rewarded you a seat in heavenly places.

Continue to be steadfast and unmovable and always abounding in the work of the Lord and you will always be victorious. Resistance to evil is proof that you fear God and not man. Soberness and vigilance kept you ahead of the calamity to come. Willingness and obedience proves to God that you are ready to eat the good of the land.

"Convince me," says the Lord, and see me open a window of heaven to bless you immeasurably. Prove to me that your worship is for real, and watch me seek you out to provide your every need. Make full proof your love for me, and I will shower you with the former and the latter rain to bring in a harvest."

You don't have to prove that you are successful in God; the proof is in your blessedness from God.

Prophetic Word For Day 47
ARISE

Arise - to get up, to move upward, mount, and ascend.[1]

It's your time and your season to arise. You've been on the bottom long enough. Get up from that place of despair and get your confidence back knowing you can do all things through Christ who strengthens you.

God said, "Arise and awake out of slumber. Didn't I say the first shall be last and last shall be first? Look (recognize) and see you are first in line. Arise and put back on your armor and take dominion in your vineyard. I have given you power to rise above every situation. You shall advance and occupy.

"Arise my sons and my daughters and put on your mantles for, I have placed my glory on you. Your mantle distinguishes your gifting and the places to which you have been called. The place to which you have been called is an elevated place and requires faith and courage. Arise I say, and again I say arise for your journey is great."

Prophetic Word For Day 48
EXPECT

Expect - to anticipate the birth of, to look forward to.[1]

God is going to blow our minds with the great expectation that we have in him. God says to expect more! If you expect one miracle, God said expect many miracles. If you expect a door to be open, God says expect many to be opened unto you. The more you expect the more God can bring forth the manifestation of that which you have anticipated.

Look forward to seeing the seeds you have sown come to full fruition in this season. God is going to take your little and make it much because you put it in the master's hand. Count on seeing God make the impossible possible. You thought he blessed you last year, but this year, anticipate the "not room enough blessing".

You are going to birth much in this season of expectation. Your faith is going to move not just mountains that have been in your way, but move God to favor you in your endeavors.

Expect more! God wants to give you more. You haven't seen anything yet. You haven't dreamed your biggest dream yet. You haven't received your greatest harvest yet, but expect it not many days hence says the Lord.

Prophetic Word For Day 49
EMPOWER

Empower - to give power or authority to[1]

God is empowering you man and woman of God to authorize the Kingdom of Heaven to govern divine things in the realm of the spirit in order to bring heaven to earth.

"I have given you access to the keys in Heaven to bind and to lose heavenly things to the I have given you power to get wealth so that you can establish my covenant in the earth. Go forth with forceful progression and advance the Kingdom. Be not fearful for I am with you. Release as much as you like from Heaven for in my government there is no end."

You have been empowered by the Greater One who is in you. He will lead you and guide you into the wealthy places.

God is going to empower our leaders with more wisdom, understanding and knowledge of spiritual things that will give them authority to delegate Kingdom business to prosper the Church. The power of God wants to engulf you, so embrace it and flow in the anointing of the Spirit.

May the power of God be with you!

Prophetic Word For Day 50
RADICAL

Radical - thoroughgoing or extreme, especially as it regards to change from accepted or traditional forms.[1]

This season you will need to take radical steps to get radical outcomes. The enemy has come against you and you should push back with the same intensity. Anticipate a greater dimension of spiritual dreams, visions, and supernatural encounters. You will be given many opportunities to reach new levels in God and see the effects of your radical changes.

God uses the foolish things to confound the wise. Therefore, it's going to take you doing something foolish and radical to get God's attention to move on your behalf. God hates traditions; He wants someone cutting edge like you to be extreme to make unprecedented changes. God is about to shake some things up in the church so much that you won't be able to recognize it.

Don't be afraid to be different. Don't be afraid to do some extreme things. Don't be afraid to change laws and traditions. Don't be afraid to lose some people, places or things. Don't be afraid to gain popularity. Don't be afraid of the sudden prosperity.

Be transformational! Be unprecedented! Be radical!

ABOUT THE AUTHOR

Prophet Kecha Chambers was set into the Office of Prophet and named House Prophet in May 2014 of the Empowerment Word & Truth Church. She is a member of the ministry team and serves under the leadership of Apostle Robbie C. Peters, Senior Leader and Apostle Sharon R. Peters, Servant Leader.

Prophet Chambers is faithful to the vision of the house and true and committed servant to the work of the Kingdom, she also serves on the Church Board of Directors, on the Board of Elders, as Head Intercessor and Head Finance Officer. Prophet Chambers was accepted into the

Kingdom of our Lord and Savior Jesus Christ in May of 2002 and ordained as Minister in 2008 and as Elder in 2011.

Prophet Chambers also serves on the Board of Directors of the Sweet Rose of Sharon's Women's Ministry, where God turned her "ashes to beauty". The excellence and anointing of this ministry has caused her light to shine and for her to come forth as a daughter of the King!

Prophet Chamber's most developed gift and first love is Intercessory Prayer. As a "warrior of prayer", she is most effective in the war room, breaking strongholds of the mind and yokes of bondage off of God's people. The demons in hell know her name! Prophet Chambers is "radical" in the spirit and powerful in the Prayer of the Word, this helps many to be loosed and set free. She has a burden to pray for the ministry and for the entire body of Christ.

Prophet Chambers is a God fearing woman who loves to praise and worship her Creator. She is "single, satisfied" and on fire for the Lord, desiring to always please Him. Prophet Chambers is pressing toward her mission to take the gospel of Jesus Christ to the nations.